Currents of Air & Age

Ruža Dabić-Bučak

First published by Busybird Publishing 2024

Copyright © 2024 Ruža Dabić-Bučak

ISBN:
Print 978-1-923216-41-9

This work is copyright. Apart from any use permitted under the *Copyright Act 1968*, no part of this publication may be reproduced, stored in a retrieval system or transmitted in any form or by any means, electronic, mechanical, photocopying, recording or otherwise, without the prior written permission of Ruža Dabić-Bučak.

The information in this book is based on the author's experiences and opinions. The author and publisher disclaim responsibility for any adverse consequences, which may result from use of the information contained herein. Permission to use any external content has been sought by the author. Any breaches will be rectified in further editions of the book.

Cover design: Busybird Publishing

Layout and typesetting: Busybird Publishing

Editor: Krystle Herdy

Busybird Publishing
2/118 Para Road
Montmorency, Victoria
Australia 3094
www.busybird.com.au

From me
To you

Contents

Summer Morning	1
Youth	2
Calm Seas + Waves = Life	3
Your Look	4
One Way	5
Anja	6
A Pearl	8
If I Were	9
My Dream	10
Knowledge	11
Ladies' Choice	12
You Are Fire, I Am Water	13
Kolonija-Šećerana Blooms, 2023	14
River Sava, Županja'S Buddy	16
Treasury	17
Super Granny	18
The Beautiful Green Danube	20
Alira	21
Eyes Wide Open	22
Worthless	24
My Slavonia	26

Snowflakes	28
Our Words	29
Poverty	30
Blue Diamond	32
Borrowing Bicycles	34
Županja, 2023	36
My Fog	37
Currents Of Air & Age	38
Ga Pre & Post	40
My Bike & I	42
The Sea Today	44
A Dawn Date	46
My Great Pleasure	47
One Word	48
My Hair	49
One More Time	50
The Value Of Life	52
The Story Of Us	53
The Last Bit	54
About The Author	56

SUMMER MORNING

This early morning,
the sea is smooth and
the sky is
drowsy
with one eye half open.

The horizon
is vague.
Is it the water's end
or the azure sky's ascent?

The sandy beach
stretches infinitely
around me.

Warm water splashes
my bare legs,
wet sand teasing
my relaxed toes.

The sun hums high.
With the taste of salt,
cool, gentle wind
caresses my face and
tousles my grey hair
to the call of morning magpies.

YOUTH

Youth is the spring of life.
It is a time of development:
physical, psychological,
emotional and social.

Obvious time of awakening,
self-awareness and an
increased desire for knowledge.

Unfolding of new personalities,
imaginations and energies,
creating long-lasting memories.

Time of running
instead of walking,
overwhelming with beauty
rather than with duty.

Happiness or disappointments
can fill each day,
along with learning, adapting,
testing and reacting.

these lessons are a ring
in the chain of life.
Youth is a most precious time,
yours, mine, ours.
Youth is the same for all of us,
such are its powers.

CALM SEAS + WAVES = LIFE

This night sky, clear,
warm and secretive.
Thousands of stars dance
to the leader-moon's charm.

The sea is calm.
It shines like a mirror,
the reflection of the moon
silent and hypnotic.

My back leans on an old pine.
Its dry needles are soft.
The scent is intoxicating,
desirable and seductive.

With your head in my lap,
my heartbeat sprints.
Your green eyes are two embers,
igniting this idyll.

I'm on a road of no return.
Path unknown
but destination
very much my own.

After half a century,
I'm still at my destination.
The night sky, the moon,
the stars are the same.

The sea (but a different one) is here.
The pine trees are here,
but the Adriatic is not
                      I fear.

YOUR LOOK

The look of your eyes—
deep, penetrating,
persistent, inquiring—
affects my heart's beating.

Your look wordlessly says
that one soul burns
about its hopes and wishes
and restless emotions.

The look, shiny and clear,
plays happy keys,
notes of peace and love
with such great ease.

The look, sharp and glaring,
thunders, aches.
Concern awakes.

Then, another look,
pained and weary
like the weather pre-rain,
heavy and teary.

The look, your look,
cloudy, broken,
bruised and sore, says
the bridge is no more.

ONE WAY

Is this music?
No, it's my voice.
Is this lightning?
No, it's the gleam in my eye.

Is that a smile?
It is.
It whispers your name.
Is that a fire?
Yes, it is the love in my heart.

Are those outstretched arms?
Yes, here to
take you into
my embrace.

Stop!

How can I erase
the sparkle in those eyes?
How do I douse
the fire in that heart?
How do I halt
outstretched arms?

I don't know,
but I have to.
I can't give
what I don't have.

Forgive me!

Your love is painful,
unlucky,
one way.

ANJA

Out of a group of three,
she came our way,
so determined,
on that beautiful day.

She sat on her little butt
and looked at us
as if to say *I chose you*
without any fuss.

Only six weeks old,
a cuddly, soft bundle
with a jet-black coat
and eyes brown as coal.

That was the start
of a love affair
between us and her,
a bond as thick as her fur.

We named her Anja,
as in Žup-*Anja*.
To me, very dear
but far, not near.

She grew into an
amazing companion.
Oh, so loyal and smart
right from the very start.

There was much
love and admiration,
from both ways,
in every moment, always.

Eleven years
was not enough.
When Anja became unwell,
the time came to say farewell.

I cradled her face and
held her gaze,
quietly giving her permission
to let go, to make that transition.

It took a double dose
to help her on her way.
As I wept, I said, 'I love you girl,
our brilliant black pearl.'

Big, round tears
rolled down her face,
and ever so gently,
she left with grace.

Losing her broke our hearts,
and they still haven't mended yet.
We still miss you, Anja;
you are a love we will never forget.

A PEARL

There is a petite pearl
named Županja.
It sits in Slavonia,
its beautiful mother shell.

In the past, Županja dazzled.
Now, not so much.
The clouds rolled over,
leaving it rather frazzled.

But dark clouds come and go;
their shadow doesn't stay.
The sun will be back
in its full glory one day.

People leave, and others come
seeking out their luck.
It's a pattern
from ever. Forever.

The sun brings wisdom,
long-needed forgiveness,
prosperity, integrity and
long-longed-for proud identity.

Županja, you glistened.
You can again.
You are a tough girl,
just like your mother of pearl.

IF I WERE

If I were a bird,
I would be a nightingale.
I would dance
in flight all night.

While chirping Strauss'
The Beautiful Blue Danube,
I would create
waltzing figure eights.

I would rest
on the twig of a bush
and sing *Ave Maria*
under magical Slavonian skies
to lighten sorrowful hearts
in need of peaceful release.

Then, at the peak of dawn,
like a tired reveller,
slowly, step by step,
I would return to my
hidden nest,
still alone but
hoping for the best.

MY DREAM

I have an acquaintance
who has been visiting me
since my childhood,
my early and mature youth.

In my declining years,
these visits are less,
so it appears.

When they occur,
I leap into the air
towards the blue sky,
then swim, not fly.

I swim breaststroke,
frontwards, backwards,
left and right.
There are no borders,
traffic lights or orders.

I, light as a feather,
always barefoot,
enchanted by calmness
and limitless blue.

This dream, every time
exactly the same,
is a faithful gift
from high above,
given to me with love.

KNOWLEDGE

Knowledge
is the light
through which we see truth,
evil and good.

It is salvation.
It drags us
from darkness,
ignorance,
slavery and misery.

Formal education is important,
but it isn't the only way.
Life is also a teacher
on the path to awareness.

Knowledge is
attainable, needed,
infinite, immense.

Our thirst for knowledge
is strong and endless.
Knowledge is our power.

LADIES' CHOICE

The band announced,
'This next dance,
ladies choose a partner.'

She took a chance,
walked to his table
and asked,
'May I have this dance?'

Amazed, he followed her
with a smile.
They danced the number.

He understood.
She was courageous.
She was defiant.
She did what she could.

An unusual battleground
was chosen wisely,
for the final round.

I don't remember
if it was a tango,
waltz or some other.
It was so long ago.

At the end
she took a deep breath and thought,
That's that.
I still have might.
I won this final fight.

YOU ARE FIRE, I AM WATER

This night is silent,
mysterious and snowy.
Not dark but a clear, blue-grey.

Thousands of snowflakes
dance a white lace
across my face.

Under my feet,
fresh snow is squeaking,
but it is you I am seeking.

Your footprints are visible.
I look up,
my heart racing.

There you are,
under the
heavily powdered tree.

Embrace me swiftly.
Kiss me.
I need your warm breath.

You are ember.
I am kindling.

KOLONIJA-ŠEĆERANA BLOOMS, 2023

You wake
slowly. Not easily.
There is glee
in your eyes.

You throw away your
worn-out clothes and
replace them without delay.

Much has gone:
two rows of poplar trees,
schools, restaurants, the library,
cinema and bowling alley;

the brass frogs
of the fountain,
the jets of water,
all destroyed.

Evening walks
are simple memories,
replaced by nights of
televisions and mobile phones.

There are no acacias,
but poplar trees still stand
along the wire fence
on the way to the river Sava.

Not many people go on foot.
A few bikes stand
here and there,
but cars are everywhere.

The hedgerows
have survived.
They are green and healthy.
The same, new and old at once.

Even many gardens
are cared for.
They are full of veggies,
flowers and fruits.

Scaffolding ornaments
a block of old flats.
The windows and shutters are changed.
Exterior walls painted.

New doors and roofs
are happily humming,
as if even they know
this change was a long time coming.

Young people are coming back.
Like beautiful flowers,
children blossom.
The estate is sobbing less.

Šećerana's residents are
hardworking and strong.
They have patiently waited
for improvement for so very long.

Šećerana, though much has changed,
you made up your mind to
bloom once more and
shine as you have before.

Kolonija-Šećerana, you were a queen.
I know you will be again.
You are gold of the highest grade.
Beauty like yours can never fade.

RIVER SAVA, ŽUPANJA'S BUDDY

The Sava is the largest tributary
of the Danube River.
She is nature's creation,
the carrier of mighty water,
vital to my nation.

She runs ceaselessly,
working zealously.

She winds around Županja
like a waltz dancer.
She shows off,
then continues on her way
in an elegant display.

When quiet and happy,
Županja adores her, but
at times, Sava is restless.
Her waters rise.
With an excited shrill,
she wishes to spill.

In those moments,
Županja and Sava
tussle in convulsive embrace;
one pushing,
the other resisting.

Rapture or rupture,
everything between
Sava and Županja
goes on forever.

Whether calm or angry,
Sava declares,
Water is life.
I am mighty.
Respect me.

TREASURY

Somewhere
deep in my soul
is a special place.

It has no address.
No house number.
None of that is needed.
This place is
not for others,
it is only for me.

Here I store
my treasures;
my memories and dreams,
whether fulfilled or not.

I named it Treasury.
It's well-protected,
with armoured walls.
The door is not locked
with a metal key or electronics;
the code is my mind.

I think each of us
holds our very own Treasury.

SUPER GRANNY

My granny was
an incredible lady.
Mara was her name, and
spoiling us was her aim.

She was illiterate
but advanced.
Well ahead of her generation;
life was her education.

She spoke few words of English
but loved Australian television.
She understood it all.
That, I clearly recall.

For our breakfasts,
Granny made pancakes,
yummy donuts or fries.
Oh, it was paradise.

She walked us to school and
taught us to play cards: Sevens.
She always had five ace sevens.
How was known only by the heavens.

There are no
granny's pancakes or
sweet strudels anymore.
Nowadays, it's only cornflakes.

I can still play Sevens,
but I still haven't learned
how to hold an extra seven
in my possession.

This lady
wasn't just any granny.
She was my very special,
always-loving super granny.
Even now, I still sense
the scent of her face
and the softness of her hands.
Even now, I feel her in every space.

THE BEAUTIFUL GREEN DANUBE

You glimmer
in the early dawn
as we sail
on and on.

I think you are
winking at me
to win me over.
That I can see.

Your eyes are green,
not blue.
Did Johann Strauss II make a mistake?
Was he not wide awake?

How green they are.

I'm sure Johann didn't err.
He knew.
He was fully aware.

Johann, Johann,
your waltz is a job well done,
but I say, when it comes to my view,
green is much nicer than blue.

ALIRA

One day last November,
a beautiful baby arrived,
much desired and longed for.
What a sight to remember.

No more waiting,
anxiety or expecting.
This special bundle of joy
is a little sister
for a gorgeous little boy.

She was named Alira
by her loving parents.
The name means
truth, beauty, freedom.
A great start, we all agree.

Baka Mira is
in seventh heaven.
She likes having Alira near
to watch and hold her dear.

Welcome, dear baby girl.
Our bright ray of light,
wanted and needed,
our shiny, precious pearl.

EYES WIDE OPEN

I am here again
with eyes wide open.
The picture I see is
different to what it used to be.

I see number 18.
Not of the sixties' Kolonija-Šećerana,
but of the present.
An altered estate Šećerana.

It is the same building but
older and unkempt.
No longer as it was before;
not young and proud anymore.

The front garden is full of weeds.
There are no flowers.
Decades of neglect
have left everything wrecked.

There is no sweet fragrance.
Our purple lilac shrub
isn't there.
All is bare.

Everything has gone.
Hyacinths, snowdrops
and powder-scented violets,
my once beautiful, loyal friends.

The place is deserted,
quiet
other than
the chirping of swallows.

They still return
to their old nest
under the eaves
at their old address.

My head spins.
My ears roar.
This sorrowful present is
nothing like what came before.

My mind begs me
to shut my eyes tight,
so that we might go back
to that happy place
where I might see
one dear, dear face.

WORTHLESS

He came home
in a dark state;
his muffled groan
known at any rate.

She was baking for Easter.
He thought her in his way.
He hit and pushed her hard
down the stairs that day.

She crawled back upstairs,
bruised and battered,
choked by tears,
pained and humiliated.

A small girl watched,
paralysed with fear,
wishing to be invisible
to the untamed bear.

The woman embraced her daughter
without a word,
trying to shield and protect her
helpless, flightless little bird.

That horrid storm
never abated.
It only changed form;
it was never sated.

*Hom*e wasn't a happy nest
for her and her chicks.
It was a trap,
financial, cultural, firm.

Unable to break out,
she shielded her offspring
from humiliation and pain
under her broken wings.

Her little flightless bird
grew and saw the light.
Towards the sun
she finally took flight.

On this marathon run,
the bird led her siblings
and her tired, much-loved mum
to her own woven nest:

big, loving and warm,
a haven from black clouds
and the horrid, violent storm.

Time and distance did their deeds,
and in the end, he was worthless,
he was a withered weed.
He was nothing. He was nameless.

MY SLAVONIA

To the right, all is green.
To the left, all is yellow.

A field of sunflowers
stands, yellow and proud.
They look towards the sun,
then shyly down when there is none.

The cornfields
are a Slavonian pride.
On the plant's top are tassels
around corn cob silks.

To the right of the road
is an oak forest with
mighty, rich and seasoned trees.
A pure wealth, everyone agrees.

The immense plains
expand indefinitely.
They meet the blue sky
at the horizon affectionately.

By a ditch,
a brown rabbit waits for his friends.
Eci-peci-pec is the game they will play
on this sunny day.

Rows of tall poplar trees
stand grandly
like soldiers at attention.
Pure perfection.

Once the wheat is harvested,
only stubble remains.

Slavonia is in my heart.
It stands resolutely, firmly.
It refuses to budge.
We are entwined eternally.

SNOWFLAKES

They landed gently
on my palm.
As soon as they fell,
they didn't dwell.

The sky is a sieve,
straining fine snowflakes.
Billions of minute pixies
weaving delicate lace with ease.

They fall in rhythm,
a waltz, Viennese or
some other,
creating a white, glistening cover.

Always six-sided
but each very different.
All mesmerising, their landings diligent.
They are all magnificent.

OUR WORDS

Potent creations
by a higher power,
versatile and adaptable.

Even just one, a single one,
can have a terrible force:
destruction or salvation,
light or darkness.

They can push one into an abyss
OR give you a helping hand.

Without words, life is unthinkable.
A word, whether
tangible, spoken or visible is
incomparable.

Without words, there is no prose, no poetry.
Our words are irreplaceable.
The value of our words is priceless.

POVERTY

Poverty, you are brutal,
indiscriminate and tireless.
You are powerful,
full of darkness.

You bathe in someone's tears
every moment
of your existence.
You are persistent, muddy, resistant.

You have always existed;
always blooming,
never getting old,
never disappearing or dying.

Poverty, you are so very generous,
happily giving
hunger, pain, sickness,
misery and helplessness.

You dance to the cries
of the poor,
laughing while you
throw salt in their eyes.

You are rigid and cruel.
You exist without a heart.
While the unfortunate are suffocating
you are loudly singing.

You rob people of hope;
kill the old and young, too.
You are not selective.
It's all the same to you.

Poverty, you steal dignity,
a basic human right
of every man
since time began.

You spread yourself
from east to west,
from north to south.

You are humanity's greatest grief,
sower of hardship and humiliation,
slavery and hopelessness.
You are a joyful thief.

When will your streak end?
When will the sun shine for all and
not just for a lucky few?
When will hope come true?

We must break your vicious cycle and
create a way out and away from you.
An entrance for all to eternal well-being
is a change that is long overdue.

BLUE DIAMOND

You, blue wonder,
agitated or calm,
are the most beautiful.
For my sore eyes, a soothing balm.

Looking at you
hypnotises me,
your pull as strong
as a lovers' song.

I soar above you
on the notes of a waltz,
barefoot and weightless,
admiring your greatness.

I absorb and engrave
the details of your
dazzling face
into my being for safekeeping.

Every inlet
is a painting
created with love
by the one from above.

Over old stone houses,
red-tiled roofs
stand like musketeers
loyally protecting,
steady at the ready.

Your crystal clear water is warm;
it caresses me.
I swim and swim.
It makes me light and free.

You are exquisite,
moving in blue but
shimmering in green.
You are the best I have ever seen.
I am not coming back.
I know this will be
my last visit.
But we'll meet again,
even if only in spirit.

Farewell.
Goodbye, my
precious Adriatic Sea.
You will always be
the blue diamond to me.

BORROWING BICYCLES

Growing up, the only two cars
in my neighbourhood
were for the sugar factory director
and our local doctor.

Even the humble bicycle was a
personal transportation
not available to everyone.

Owning a bike was a rarity
in my small
Slavonian estate.

If you had a bike,
you were important…
and usually male.

We didn't have phones.
All our business was done
personally, face to face.

We walked everywhere;
to the shops, to the pharmacy,
to get a priest.
Walking, one foot in front of the other,
step-by-step over great distances
was the only way for us.

At the time, bicycle borrowing
was common.
For many, it was a necessary
but painful shame.

It wasn't easy.
Some wouldn't lend their bikes
but you still had to ask.

Those who lent their bikes
and helped others in need
earned great respect.
My father had a bike.
It was sacred to him and
never once borrowed out.

In time, my mama
bought a bike of her own,
a second-hand, scuffed-blue,
steel-wheeled steed,
and it was gladly lent
to anyone who asked.

My mother's worn-out bike was
used and appreciated by all.
Everyone knew,
if you had a bike,
you were important.
My mother
was important, but

Mama didn't need a bicycle
for me to know that.
She was kind, selfless and loving.
She was my teacher,
my hero,
my mum.

ŽUPANJA, 2023

I am here to see you again.
To absorb the old and new
and to whisper,
I still love you.

I feel your breath
and smell the scent of your streets.
I hear your heartbeat;
like my own, it is neat and sweet.

Your coffee is good,
as is your strawberry ice cream,
but your bread is the champion.
For me, it's number one.

There is a new phenomenon.
Cafes are all around,
and they're visited from dawn
'til late, I've found.

Friends and acquaintances meet.
They talk over long coffee.
Personal, sports and political problems
they solve, and many sins they absolve.

Županja, I admire the shade
of your trees,
just as I did so long ago.
I love and enjoy it all with ease.

Županja, you are beautiful,
but so much has changed.
But I guess that's normal,
because just as I have,
your streets have aged.

MY FOG

Invisible fog,
you are heavy.
I am groaning.
I am choking.

I can't see the way.
I am stuck
right here;
I do not wish to stay.

I move forward;
nothing changes.
I reverse, and
you stop me by force.

All is concealed.
The distance is difficult to phantom.
I don't know
how to proceed.

You are grey.
You are unkind.
You are rough.
You are tough.

I want out
of this confusion
and into clarity
without a doubt.

I am lost.
Go away, my fog.
I need to find myself
before my soul turns to frost.

CURRENTS OF AIR & AGE

The wind of aging has
taken away the
beauty of youth.
Your speed has gone;
your strength and six-pack, too.
Your stoic endurance
is interrupted by
after-lunch rest, but
old age commands this simple request.

You don't dance much
these days,
blaming your stillness on
new knees.
And though your interest in
travelling has paled,
you still do,
because you know I need you.

Not all has changed.

Your deep green eyes,
your warm lips, your gentle touch,
all still constant and
desired so very much.

The feel of your skin
remains the same,
as does its scent.
The you that I am drawn to
is still very much present.

You are my home, my
happy harbour, in days
both old and new.
Simply put,
as long as the winds keep raging,
I will always
love you.

GA PRE & POST

A few butterflies
in my stomach,
and my chest's slow rise
are my muffled cries.

Regardless of the number
of times I've
had it before,
it's always a bummer.

Is it fear?
I pretend not,
but the feeling
is there, very near.

I trust them.
I need them.
So, go ahead;
yes, please.

With a little sting,
the cannula went in,
and the Doc said,
we can begin.

It felt cold
as she pushed
some meds in,
just as I was told.

My last thought was,
'Oh, how easy
this would be
to set one free.'

Total weightlessness
took me gently
away into
nothingness.

I opened my eyes.
Already? All done?
Any problems?
No, none.

MY BIKE & I

Cool breaths of fresh air
touch my face
before drifting and lifting
my grey hair with flair.

It is like a dream
to be up here
on my bike again,
riding without fear.

Titanium bits
in my old spine
kept me careful, so, of
bike riding, I became fearful.

But today,
I don't know why,
I hopped on my old wheels
for a ride without a sigh.

I feel free
as a bird,
forgetting my age.
What a change.

This dear bike
and me, both now old,
are a team, once again
happy on the road.

Hey, you gorgeous
magical breeze,
you help me
ride my bike with ease.

I want to throw
my arms in the air,
so my bike and I
can fly high without a care.

THE SEA TODAY

Today, this Australian sea
is grey-green.
It's rough, frothy,
angry and haughty.
It is changed, but beautiful.

This is its other face.
It warns me,
grabs my gaze,
taking it to
the left,   the right,
then straight ahead.

The horizon is
a little uncertain.
It is the end
and the beginning
of the sky's curtains.

There is nobody out there.
Nothing.
No boats.
No fishermen.

Only one tanker is
brave enough to get close,
carrying oil to Geelong,
navigating the sea respectfully.

The sea is howling;
a warning,
a comfort
of the beginning and the end.

A DAWN DATE

I greet the white swans,
up early,
wide-eyed and free,
happy like me.

They are graceful beauties
gliding on the river Main,
bathed in early, orange sun.
Pure elegance, having great fun.

Do they swim
to the tune of a waltz
or a gentle tango?
I can't say, but I watch them go.

Their moves are majestic
and oh so elegant.
They are so sweet,
perfect and neat.

A higher power
gifted their grace to us
to enrich our world
with beauty and no fuss.

MY GREAT PLEASURE

I am standing here, you
caressing me gently
but deliberately.
Your hot touch
makes me relax considerably.

Deep sighs of bliss,
loyal and grateful,
escape my throat
without a miss.

Oh, how heavenly
is this feeling of joy?
Many take it for granted,
but they should not.

Your touch is a precious commodity,
an immense and important novelty.
My greatest pleasure, my greatest power
will always be my nice, hot shower.

ONE WORD

The light went out
with one word/
a quiet word, not a shout.
All is blurred.

I am falling,
not fighting it, and
with bitter tears shedding,
I've ended in a pit.

Here's where I'll stay.
It's the right place;
on this dark day,
I will vanish without a trace.

Out there are sun, rain and snow;
there are books, music and dance.
They plead, *You are needed.*
Come out and give us a chance.

MY HAIR

Where is my lovely hair?
Where? Where?
It ran away,
leaving me bald and in despair.

My new hair,
soft as silk,
is growing shyly
but beautifully. Visibly.

This new hair is
like a duckling's down;
it's very precious,
leaving me happily breathless.

Here is my new hair.
New hair.
I wear it with flair.
Do not stare!

ONE MORE TIME

I am standing
on our street
in the old town
where we walked tirelessly
and enjoyed the sea happily.

A lot has changed.
These houses are
not like our old, stone ones.
With time, change comes.

The roofs are no longer red,
but colourless and flat.
It appears as though these houses
stand without a hat.

Also, the Riva is not the same.
Most of the benches
and pines are missing,
leaving me reminiscing,

but ours is still here, waiting
for me to return
from far away
and visit today.

This is where we kissed
for the first time.
Many promises were made,
but many were not kept, I am afraid.

Now, I sit alone
under our pine tree,
absorbing the beauty
of this beautiful sea.

I am enchanted.
The breeze takes me
on its wings and carries me
towards the sunset.
Dark blue below,
bright red above,
the tired sunset whispers,
I send you my love.

I blink and feel
a breath on my face.
Am I alone?
Do I need to atone?

I am grateful
for this, this
one more time. Just one,
but one is better than none.

THE VALUE OF LIFE

Life is life.
It flows, but how
depends on
which way it goes.

Is life just?
No, it never is.
It caresses and loves some while
neglecting and beating others.

Life can be
materially rich
but poor intellectually,
crippled humanly.

Whether life is
rich or poor,
most still love it.
We all find our fit.

Every life, every single one,
whether grand and adorned in gold
or rough and helplessly poor,
is precious.
Every life equally matters.

THE STORY OF US

You stood on the ship's deck,
deep in thought,
looking at the blue sea
that brought you to me.

When you turned to meet my gaze,
I knew that we were one.
Like me, I knew you knew
our journey had begun.

You are my food, my water,
my sun and my air, and
on days when I am weak,
it is always you I seek.

You are my calm, safe harbour,
I am your sea-swept boat,
and though storms and sprays may rage us,
you are the peace in which I float.

You say life just wouldn't be worth it;
without this Slavonian seagull, you'd be done.
But the truth is, the story of us
is that you and I are one.

THE LAST BIT

How much of my path
do I have left to walk?
Is there long to go?
It's a secret only life knows.

More and more often
these days
the same thought
grazes my mind.

There is no inkling,
no warning to prepare.
No one tells you about the
end of your path,
the when or even the where.

I am aware
it's coming.
It comes to all.
Sometimes, I feel it near.

Will crossing
from here to there
be easy or tough?
Will it be long or just
one short puff?

Will it fade
like the end of
a favourite song or
go out loud with the
sound of a gong?

Will it hurt?
Will I refuse to go,
desperately trying
to stay,
kicking and screaming?

Will anyone hold my hand,
kiss my cheek
and gently say,
'Let go, it's OK.'

Will my mum be there
to help me
find my way
on that final day?

Perhaps there is a meadow
full of wildflowers
for me to run barefoot
or waltz in for many hours.

I have too many questions,
as always,
but not long to go.
This is my last phase.

There is justice
in not knowing,
when or how
one is going.

The end is the same
for us all,
poor or rich,
big or small.

'Til then, I will go on
reading, writing,
dancing and loving.
Walking slowly
but not running.

About the Author

Ruža Dabić-Bučak was born in Croatia in 1950 and grew up in her much-loved Kolonija, Šećerana, Županja.

Ruža and her husband immigrated to Melbourne, Australia, in 1971, where they still live with their family.

A retired oncology clinical nurse consultant, Ruža came to poetry late in life, writing her first poems just two days before her 60th birthday. She writes in both English and Croatian.

Currents of Air & Age is Ruža's second collection of poetry in English.

www.ingramcontent.com/pod-product-compliance
Lightning Source LLC
Chambersburg PA
CBHW041301240426
43661CB00010B/981